THIS BOOK BELONGS TO:

_____

_____

_____

JESUS LOVES ME

Jesus loves me! This I know,
For the Bible tells me so;
Little ones to Him belong;
They are weak, but He is strong.

Refrain:
Yes, Jesus loves me!
Yes, Jesus loves me!
Yes, Jesus loves me!
The Bible tells me so.

THE LORD'S PRAYER

Our Father, who art in heaven,
hallowed be thy Name,
thy kingdom come,
thy will be done,
on earth as it is in heaven.

Give us this day our daily bread.
And forgive us our trespasses,
as we forgive those
who trespass against us.

And lead us not into temptation,
but deliver us from evil.

For thine is the kingdom,
and the power, and the glory,
for ever and ever. Amen.

HI, GOD!

Date _____

Today I... _____

_____

_____

_____

_____

Today I am thankful for... _____

_____

_____

_____

_____

Today I'd like to pray for... _____

_____

_____

_____

_____

AMEN!

HI, GOD!   Date _____

Today I... _____

_____

_____

_____

_____

Today I am thankful for... _____

_____

_____

_____

_____

Today I'd like to pray for... _____

_____

_____

_____

_____

AMEN!

HI, GOD!

Date _____

Today I... _____

_____

_____

_____

_____

Today I am thankful for... _____

_____

_____

_____

_____

Today I'd like to pray for... _____

_____

_____

_____

_____

AMEN!

HI, GOD!

Date _____

Today I... _____

_____

_____

_____

_____

Today I am thankful for... _____

_____

_____

_____

_____

Today I'd like to pray for... _____

_____

_____

_____

_____

AMEN!

HI, GOD!

Date _____

Today I... _____

_____

_____

_____

_____

Today I am thankful for... _____

_____

_____

_____

_____

Today I'd like to pray for... _____

_____

_____

_____

_____

AMEN!

HI, GOD!

Date _____

Today I... _____

_____

_____

_____

_____

Today I am thankful for... _____

_____

_____

_____

_____

Today I'd like to pray for... _____

_____

_____

_____

_____

AMEN!

HI, GOD!

Date _____

Today I... _____
_____
_____
_____
_____

Today I am thankful for... _____
_____
_____
_____
_____

Today I'd like to pray for... _____
_____
_____
_____
_____

AMEN!

HI, GOD!

Date _____

Today I... _____

_____

_____

_____

_____

Today I am thankful for... _____

_____

_____

_____

Today I'd like to pray for... _____

_____

_____

_____

_____

AMEN!

HI, GOD!

Date _____

Today I... _____
_____
_____
_____
_____

Today I am thankful for... _____
_____
_____
_____

Today I'd like to pray for... _____
_____
_____
_____
_____

AMEN!

HI, GOD!

Date _____

Today I... _____

_____

_____

_____

_____

Today I am thankful for... _____

_____

_____

_____

_____

Today I'd like to pray for... _____

_____

_____

_____

_____

AMEN!

HI, GOD!

Date _____

Today I... _____

_____

_____

_____

_____

Today I am thankful for... _____

_____

_____

_____

_____

Today I'd like to pray for... _____

_____

_____

_____

_____

AMEN!

HI, GOD!

Date _____

Today I... _____

_____

_____

_____

_____

Today I am thankful for... _____

_____

_____

_____

_____

Today I'd like to pray for... _____

_____

_____

_____

_____

AMEN!

HI, GOD!

Date _____

Today I... _____

_____

_____

_____

_____

Today I am thankful for... _____

_____

_____

_____

_____

Today I'd like to pray for... _____

_____

_____

_____

_____

AMEN!

HI, GOD! Date _____

Today I... _____

_____

_____

_____

_____

Today I am thankful for... _____

_____

_____

_____

_____

Today I'd like to pray for... _____

_____

_____

_____

_____

AMEN!

HI, GOD!

Date _____

Today I... _____

_____

_____

_____

_____

Today I am thankful for... _____

_____

_____

_____

_____

Today I'd like to pray for... _____

_____

_____

_____

_____

AMEN!

HI, GOD!

Date _____

Today I... _____

_____

_____

_____

_____

Today I am thankful for... _____

_____

_____

_____

_____

Today I'd like to pray for... _____

_____

_____

_____

_____

AMEN!

HI, GOD!

Date _____

Today I... _____

_____

_____

_____

_____

Today I am thankful for... _____

_____

_____

_____

_____

Today I'd like to pray for... _____

_____

_____

_____

_____

AMEN!

HI, GOD!

Date _____

Today I... _____

_____

_____

_____

_____

Today I am thankful for... _____

_____

_____

_____

_____

Today I'd like to pray for... _____

_____

_____

_____

_____

AMEN!

HI, GOD!

Date _____

Today I... _____

_____

_____

_____

_____

Today I am thankful for... _____

_____

_____

_____

_____

Today I'd like to pray for... _____

_____

_____

_____

_____

AMEN!

HI, GOD!

Date _____

Today I... _____

_____

_____

_____

_____

Today I am thankful for... _____

_____

_____

_____

_____

Today I'd like to pray for... _____

_____

_____

_____

_____

AMEN!

HI, GOD!   Date _____

Today I... _____

_____

_____

_____

_____

Today I am thankful for... _____

_____

_____

_____

_____

Today I'd like to pray for... _____

_____

_____

_____

_____

AMEN!

HI, GOD!

Date _____

Today I... _____

_____

_____

_____

_____

Today I am thankful for... _____

_____

_____

_____

_____

Today I'd like to pray for... _____

_____

_____

_____

_____

AMEN!

HI, GOD!

Date _____

Today I... _____

_____

_____

_____

_____

Today I am thankful for... _____

_____

_____

_____

_____

Today I'd like to pray for... _____

_____

_____

_____

_____

AMEN!

HI, GOD!

Date _____

Today I... _____

_____

_____

_____

_____

Today I am thankful for... _____

_____

_____

_____

_____

Today I'd like to pray for... _____

_____

_____

_____

_____

AMEN!

HI, GOD!

Date _____

Today I... _____

_____

_____

_____

_____

Today I am thankful for... _____

_____

_____

_____

_____

Today I'd like to pray for... _____

_____

_____

_____

_____

AMEN!

HI, GOD!　Date _____

Today I... _____

_____

_____

_____

_____

Today I am thankful for... _____

_____

_____

_____

_____

Today I'd like to pray for... _____

_____

_____

_____

_____

AMEN!

HI, GOD!

Date _____

Today I... _____

_____

_____

_____

_____

Today I am thankful for... _____

_____

_____

_____

Today I'd like to pray for... _____

_____

_____

_____

AMEN!

HI, GOD!

Date _____

Today I... _____

_____

_____

_____

_____

Today I am thankful for... _____

_____

_____

_____

Today I'd like to pray for... _____

_____

_____

_____

AMEN!

HI, GOD!

Date _____

Today I... _____

_____

_____

_____

_____

Today I am thankful for... _____

_____

_____

_____

_____

Today I'd like to pray for... _____

_____

_____

_____

_____

AMEN!

HI, GOD!

Date _____

Today I... _____

_____

_____

_____

_____

Today I am thankful for... _____

_____

_____

_____

_____

Today I'd like to pray for... _____

_____

_____

_____

_____

AMEN!

HI, GOD!

Date _____

Today I... _____

_____

_____

_____

_____

Today I am thankful for... _____

_____

_____

_____

_____

Today I'd like to pray for... _____

_____

_____

_____

_____

AMEN!

HI, GOD!

Date _____

Today I... _____

_____

_____

_____

_____

Today I am thankful for... _____

_____

_____

_____

_____

Today I'd like to pray for... _____

_____

_____

_____

_____

AMEN!

HI, GOD!

Date _____

Today I... _____

_____

_____

_____

_____

Today I am thankful for... _____

_____

_____

_____

_____

Today I'd like to pray for... _____

_____

_____

_____

_____

AMEN!

HI, GOD!

Date _____

Today I... _____

_____

_____

_____

_____

Today I am thankful for... _____

_____

_____

_____

_____

Today I'd like to pray for... _____

_____

_____

_____

_____

AMEN!

HI, GOD!   Date _____

Today I... _____

_____

_____

_____

_____

Today I am thankful for... _____

_____

_____

_____

_____

Today I'd like to pray for... _____

_____

_____

_____

_____

AMEN!

HI, GOD!

Date _____

Today I... _____

_____

_____

_____

_____

Today I am thankful for... _____

_____

_____

_____

_____

Today I'd like to pray for... _____

_____

_____

_____

_____

AMEN!

HI, GOD!

Date _____

Today I... _____

_____

_____

_____

_____

Today I am thankful for... _____

_____

_____

_____

_____

Today I'd like to pray for... _____

_____

_____

_____

_____

AMEN!

HI, GOD!

Date _____

Today I... _____

_____

_____

_____

_____

Today I am thankful for... _____

_____

_____

_____

_____

Today I'd like to pray for... _____

_____

_____

_____

_____

AMEN!

HI, GOD!

Date _____

Today I... _____

_____

_____

_____

_____

Today I am thankful for... _____

_____

_____

_____

_____

Today I'd like to pray for... _____

_____

_____

_____

_____

AMEN!

HI, GOD!   Date _____

Today I... _____

_____

_____

_____

_____

Today I am thankful for... _____

_____

_____

_____

_____

Today I'd like to pray for... _____

_____

_____

_____

_____

AMEN!

HI, GOD!

Date _____

Today I... _____

_____

_____

_____

_____

Today I am thankful for... _____

_____

_____

_____

_____

Today I'd like to pray for... _____

_____

_____

_____

_____

AMEN!

HI, GOD!

Date _____

Today I... _____

_____

_____

_____

_____

Today I am thankful for... _____

_____

_____

_____

_____

Today I'd like to pray for... _____

_____

_____

_____

_____

AMEN!

HI, GOD!

Date _____

Today I... _____

_____

_____

_____

_____

Today I am thankful for... _____

_____

_____

_____

_____

Today I'd like to pray for... _____

_____

_____

_____

_____

AMEN!

HI, GOD!

Date _____

Today I... _____

_____

_____

_____

_____

Today I am thankful for... _____

_____

_____

_____

Today I'd like to pray for... _____

_____

_____

_____

_____

AMEN!

HI, GOD!

Date _____

Today I... _____

_____

_____

_____

_____

Today I am thankful for... _____

_____

_____

_____

_____

Today I'd like to pray for... _____

_____

_____

_____

_____

AMEN!

HI, GOD!   Date _____

Today I... _____

_____

_____

_____

_____

Today I am thankful for... _____

_____

_____

_____

_____

Today I'd like to pray for... _____

_____

_____

_____

_____

AMEN!

HI, GOD!

Date _____

Today I... _____

_____

_____

_____

_____

Today I am thankful for... _____

_____

_____

_____

_____

Today I'd like to pray for... _____

_____

_____

_____

_____

AMEN!

HI, GOD!

Date _____

Today I... _____

_____

_____

_____

_____

Today I am thankful for... _____

_____

_____

_____

_____

Today I'd like to pray for... _____

_____

_____

_____

_____

AMEN!

HI, GOD!

Date _____

Today I... _____

_____

_____

_____

_____

Today I am thankful for... _____

_____

_____

_____

_____

Today I'd like to pray for... _____

_____

_____

_____

_____

AMEN!

HI, GOD!

Date _____

Today I... _____

_____

_____

_____

_____

Today I am thankful for... _____

_____

_____

_____

_____

Today I'd like to pray for... _____

_____

_____

_____

AMEN!

HI, GOD!

Date _____

Today I... _____

_____

_____

_____

_____

Today I am thankful for... _____

_____

_____

_____

_____

Today I'd like to pray for... _____

_____

_____

_____

_____

AMEN!

HI, GOD!

Date _____

Today I... _____

_____

_____

_____

_____

Today I am thankful for... _____

_____

_____

_____

_____

Today I'd like to pray for... _____

_____

_____

_____

_____

AMEN!

HI, GOD!

Date _____

Today I... _____

_____

_____

_____

_____

Today I am thankful for... _____

_____

_____

_____

_____

Today I'd like to pray for... _____

_____

_____

_____

_____

AMEN!

HI, GOD!

Date _____

Today I... _____

_____

_____

_____

_____

Today I am thankful for... _____

_____

_____

_____

_____

Today I'd like to pray for... _____

_____

_____

_____

_____

AMEN!

HI, GOD!

Date _____

Today I... _____

_____

_____

_____

_____

Today I am thankful for... _____

_____

_____

_____

_____

Today I'd like to pray for... _____

_____

_____

_____

_____

AMEN!

HI, GOD!

Date _____

Today I... _____

_____

_____

_____

_____

Today I am thankful for... _____

_____

_____

_____

_____

Today I'd like to pray for... _____

_____

_____

_____

_____

AMEN!

HI, GOD!

Date _____

Today I... _____

_____

_____

_____

_____

Today I am thankful for... _____

_____

_____

_____

_____

Today I'd like to pray for... _____

_____

_____

_____

_____

AMEN!

HI, GOD!

Date _____

Today I... _____

_____

_____

_____

_____

Today I am thankful for... _____

_____

_____

_____

_____

Today I'd like to pray for... _____

_____

_____

_____

_____

AMEN!

HI, GOD!

Date _____

Today I... _____

_____

_____

_____

_____

Today I am thankful for... _____

_____

_____

_____

_____

Today I'd like to pray for... _____

_____

_____

_____

_____

AMEN!

HI, GOD!

Date _____

Today I... _____

_____

_____

_____

_____

Today I am thankful for... _____

_____

_____

_____

_____

Today I'd like to pray for... _____

_____

_____

_____

_____

AMEN!

HI, GOD!

Date _____

Today I... _____

_____

_____

_____

_____

Today I am thankful for... _____

_____

_____

_____

_____

Today I'd like to pray for... _____

_____

_____

_____

_____

AMEN!

HI, GOD!

Date _____

Today I... _____

_____

_____

_____

_____

Today I am thankful for... _____

_____

_____

_____

_____

Today I'd like to pray for... _____

_____

_____

_____

_____

AMEN!

HI, GOD!

Date _____

Today I... _____

_____

_____

_____

_____

Today I am thankful for... _____

_____

_____

_____

_____

Today I'd like to pray for... _____

_____

_____

_____

_____

AMEN!

HI, GOD!   Date _____

Today I... _____

_____

_____

_____

_____

Today I am thankful for... _____

_____

_____

_____

_____

Today I'd like to pray for... _____

_____

_____

_____

_____

AMEN!

HI, GOD!

Date _____

Today I... _____

_____

_____

_____

_____

Today I am thankful for... _____

_____

_____

_____

_____

Today I'd like to pray for... _____

_____

_____

_____

_____

AMEN!

HI, GOD!

Date _____

Today I... _____

_____

_____

_____

_____

Today I am thankful for... _____

_____

_____

_____

_____

Today I'd like to pray for... _____

_____

_____

_____

_____

AMEN!

HI, GOD!

Date _____

Today I... _____

_____

_____

_____

_____

Today I am thankful for... _____

_____

_____

_____

_____

Today I'd like to pray for... _____

_____

_____

_____

_____

AMEN!

HI, GOD!

Date _____

Today I... _____

_____

_____

_____

_____

Today I am thankful for... _____

_____

_____

_____

_____

Today I'd like to pray for... _____

_____

_____

_____

_____

AMEN!

HI, GOD!

Date _____

Today I... _____

_____

_____

_____

_____

Today I am thankful for... _____

_____

_____

_____

_____

Today I'd like to pray for... _____

_____

_____

_____

_____

AMEN!

HI, GOD!

Date _____

Today I... _____

_____

_____

_____

_____

Today I am thankful for... _____

_____

_____

_____

_____

Today I'd like to pray for... _____

_____

_____

_____

_____

AMEN!

HI, GOD!

Date _____

Today I... _____

_____

_____

_____

_____

Today I am thankful for... _____

_____

_____

_____

_____

Today I'd like to pray for... _____

_____

_____

_____

_____

AMEN!

HI, GOD!   Date _____

Today I... _____

_____

_____

_____

_____

Today I am thankful for... _____

_____

_____

_____

_____

Today I'd like to pray for... _____

_____

_____

_____

_____

AMEN!

HI, GOD!

Date _____

Today I... _____

_____

_____

_____

_____

Today I am thankful for... _____

_____

_____

_____

_____

Today I'd like to pray for... _____

_____

_____

_____

_____

AMEN!

HI, GOD!

Date _____

Today I... _____

_____

_____

_____

_____

Today I am thankful for... _____

_____

_____

_____

_____

Today I'd like to pray for... _____

_____

_____

_____

_____

AMEN!

HI, GOD!

Date _____

Today I... _____

_____

_____

_____

_____

Today I am thankful for... _____

_____

_____

_____

Today I'd like to pray for... _____

_____

_____

_____

AMEN!

HI, GOD!

Date _____

Today I... _____

_____

_____

_____

_____

Today I am thankful for... _____

_____

_____

_____

_____

Today I'd like to pray for... _____

_____

_____

_____

_____

AMEN!

HI, GOD!

Date _____

Today I... _____

_____

_____

_____

_____

Today I am thankful for... _____

_____

_____

_____

_____

Today I'd like to pray for... _____

_____

_____

_____

_____

AMEN!

HI, GOD!

Date _____

Today I... _____

_____

_____

_____

_____

Today I am thankful for... _____

_____

_____

_____

_____

Today I'd like to pray for... _____

_____

_____

_____

_____

AMEN!

HI, GOD!

Date _____

Today I... _____

_____

_____

_____

_____

Today I am thankful for... _____

_____

_____

_____

_____

Today I'd like to pray for... _____

_____

_____

_____

_____

AMEN!

HI, GOD!

Date _____

Today I... _____

_____

_____

_____

_____

Today I am thankful for... _____

_____

_____

_____

_____

Today I'd like to pray for... _____

_____

_____

_____

_____

AMEN!

HI, GOD!

Date _____

Today I... _____

_____

_____

_____

_____

Today I am thankful for... _____

_____

_____

_____

_____

Today I'd like to pray for... _____

_____

_____

_____

_____

AMEN!

HI, GOD!

Date _____

Today I... _____

_____

_____

_____

_____

Today I am thankful for... _____

_____

_____

_____

_____

Today I'd like to pray for... _____

_____

_____

_____

_____

AMEN!

HI, GOD!

Date _____

Today I... _____

_____

_____

_____

_____

Today I am thankful for... _____

_____

_____

_____

_____

Today I'd like to pray for... _____

_____

_____

_____

_____

AMEN!

HI, GOD!

Date _____

Today I... _____

_____

_____

_____

_____

Today I am thankful for... _____

_____

_____

_____

_____

Today I'd like to pray for... _____

_____

_____

_____

_____

AMEN!

HI, GOD!

Date _____

Today I... _____

_____

_____

_____

_____

Today I am thankful for... _____

_____

_____

_____

_____

Today I'd like to pray for... _____

_____

_____

_____

_____

AMEN!

HI, GOD!

Date _____

Today I... _____

_____

_____

_____

_____

Today I am thankful for... _____

_____

_____

_____

_____

Today I'd like to pray for... _____

_____

_____

_____

_____

AMEN!

HI, GOD!

Date _____

Today I... _____

_____

_____

_____

_____

Today I am thankful for... _____

_____

_____

_____

_____

Today I'd like to pray for... _____

_____

_____

_____

_____

AMEN!

HI, GOD!   Date _____

Today I... _____

_____

_____

_____

_____

Today I am thankful for... _____

_____

_____

_____

_____

Today I'd like to pray for... _____

_____

_____

_____

_____

AMEN!

HI, GOD!

Date _____

Today I... _____

_____

_____

_____

_____

Today I am thankful for... _____

_____

_____

_____

_____

Today I'd like to pray for... _____

_____

_____

_____

_____

AMEN!

HI, GOD!

Date _____

Today I... _____

_____

_____

_____

_____

Today I am thankful for... _____

_____

_____

_____

_____

Today I'd like to pray for... _____

_____

_____

_____

_____

AMEN!

HI, GOD!

Date _____

Today I... _____

_____

_____

_____

_____

Today I am thankful for... _____

_____

_____

_____

_____

Today I'd like to pray for... _____

_____

_____

_____

_____

AMEN!

HI, GOD!

Date _____

Today I... _____

_____

_____

_____

_____

Today I am thankful for... _____

_____

_____

_____

_____

Today I'd like to pray for... _____

_____

_____

_____

_____

AMEN!

HI, GOD!

Date _____

Today I... _____

_____

_____

_____

_____

Today I am thankful for... _____

_____

_____

_____

_____

Today I'd like to pray for... _____

_____

_____

_____

_____

AMEN!

HI, GOD!

Date _____

Today I... _____

_____

_____

_____

_____

Today I am thankful for... _____

_____

_____

_____

_____

Today I'd like to pray for... _____

_____

_____

_____

_____

AMEN!

HI, GOD!

Date _____

Today I... _____

_____

_____

_____

_____

Today I am thankful for... _____

_____

_____

_____

_____

Today I'd like to pray for... _____

_____

_____

_____

_____

AMEN!

HI, GOD!

Date _____

Today I... _____

_____

_____

_____

_____

Today I am thankful for... _____

_____

_____

_____

_____

Today I'd like to pray for... _____

_____

_____

_____

_____

AMEN!

HI, GOD!

Date _____

Today I... _____

_____

_____

_____

_____

Today I am thankful for... _____

_____

_____

_____

_____

Today I'd like to pray for... _____

_____

_____

_____

_____

AMEN!

HI, GOD!

Date _____

Today I... _____

_____

_____

_____

_____

Today I am thankful for... _____

_____

_____

_____

_____

Today I'd like to pray for... _____

_____

_____

_____

_____

AMEN!

HI, GOD!

Date _____

Today I... _____

_____

_____

_____

_____

Today I am thankful for... _____

_____

_____

_____

_____

Today I'd like to pray for... _____

_____

_____

_____

_____

AMEN!

HI, GOD!

Date _____

Today I... _____

_____

_____

_____

_____

Today I am thankful for... _____

_____

_____

_____

_____

Today I'd like to pray for... _____

_____

_____

_____

_____

AMEN!

HI, GOD!

Date _____

Today I... _____

_____

_____

_____

_____

Today I am thankful for... _____

_____

_____

_____

_____

Today I'd like to pray for... _____

_____

_____

_____

_____

AMEN!

HI, GOD!

Date _____

Today I... _____

_____

_____

_____

_____

Today I am thankful for... _____

_____

_____

_____

_____

Today I'd like to pray for... _____

_____

_____

_____

_____

AMEN!

HI, GOD!

Date _____

Today I... _____

_____

_____

_____

_____

Today I am thankful for... _____

_____

_____

_____

Today I'd like to pray for... _____

_____

_____

_____

AMEN!

HI, GOD!

Date _____

Today I... _____

_____

_____

_____

_____

Today I am thankful for... _____

_____

_____

_____

_____

Today I'd like to pray for... _____

_____

_____

_____

_____

AMEN!

I AM A CHILD OF

GOD

Made in the USA
Columbia, SC
02 August 2019